Aqua Planet

Poetic Seascapes and Riverscapes

Aqua Planet

Poetic Seascapes and Riverscapes

Philip Comfort

RESOURCE *Publications* • Eugene, Oregon

Resource Publications
A division of Wipf and Stock Publishers
199 W 8th Ave, Suite 3
Eugene, OR 97401

Aqua Planet
Poetic Seascapes and Riverscapes
By Comfort, Philip Wesley

ISBN 13: 978-1-61097-146-1
Publication date 4/1/2015
Previously published by Hidden Book Press, 2010

To Georgia

The love of my life

Seascapes

1. this is my ink – *p. 1*
2a. twin epiphanies – *p. 2*
2b. wet wild wind – *p. 3*
3a. seaside drum circle – *p. 4*
3b. sacred motion – *p. 5*
4a. riding giants in Hawaii – *p. 6*
4b. He'e nalu--Hawaiian surfer – *p. 7*
5a. watching my son surf – *p. 8*
5b. looking at my son surf – *p. 9*
6a. pristine waves – *p. 10*
6b. longest ride – *p. 11*
7a. between sea and cemetery – *p. 12*
7b. quick life – *p. 13*
8a. caught up in the catch – *p. 14*
8b. seaside soccer – *p. 15*
9a. looking for a long right – *p. 16*
9b. waves' faces – *p. 17*
10a. what the sea sees – *p. 18*
10b. this moment – *p. 19*
11a. the voice – *p. 20*
11b. the voice again – *p. 21*
12a. wave watchers – *p. 22*
12b. surfers – *p. 23*
13a. sleek quick runs – *p. 24*
13b. sweet smooth sunned froth – *p. 25*
14a. twilight surf – *p. 26*
14b. gusts off the Outerbanks – *p. 27*
15a. rolled waves – *p. 28*
15b. dawn intruder – *p. 29*
16a. the beach is his – *p. 30*
16b. dogangel – *p. 31*
17a. mounting moving waters – *p. 32*
17b. take me down – *p. 33*

18a. earthrise sun – *p. 34*
18b. perfect day – *p. 35*
19a. I return like morning to the sea – *p. 36*
19b. sea-spawn – *p. 37*
20a. hummingbird in hurricane – *p. 38*
20b. brute beast – *p. 39*
21a. September surf – *p. 40*
21b. broken open ocean – *p. 41*
22a. "aniphany" – *p. 42*
22b. dolphin dawn – *p. 43*
23a. ocean oaks – *p. 44*
23b. sea acacia – *p. 45*
24a. I am sea – *p. 46*
24b. Had I been chaos – *p. 47*
25a. the breathing speaking sea – *p. 48*
25b. listen to the sea – *p. 49*
26a. shadow catcher – *p. 50*
26b. spiritual soul – *p. 51*
27a. ocean incantation – *p. 52*
27b. the sea also rises – *p. 53*
28a. aqua planet – *p. 54*
28b. ride the heave – *p. 55*
29a. edge of the sea – *p. 56*
29b. visit to the seaside – *p. 57*
30a. mystical migration – *p. 58*
30b. unscrolled voyage – *p.60*
30c. invisible feel – *p. 61*
31. Boxing Day Tsunami – *p. 62*

Riverscapes

32a. between the river and the sea – *p. 74*
32b. roll Spirit, river my soul – *p. 75*
33a. slow beauty, slow circle – *p. 76*
33b. going to seed – *p. 77*
34a. catch the meaning – *p. 78*
34b. a certain presence – *p. 79*
35a. speak peace – *p. 80*
35b. watersound – *p. 81*
36a. depths – *p. 82*
36b. descent – *p. 83*
37a. visions of rivers – *p. 84*
37b. midwest streams, dolphin dreams – *p. 85*
38a. Chicora speaks – *p. 86*
38b. Black Elk speaks – *p. 87*
39a. papyrus maker – *p. 88*
39b. Ezekiel's vision – *p. 89*
40. summer has run rivers into ocean – *p. 92*

Author Biographical Notes – *p. 95*

Preface

This aqua planet is alive with seas and rivers. Nearly every poem in this volume was inspired by an actual place on the sea's edge or riverside, as the subtitles of many poems indicate. The ocean poems travel from the Pacific to the Atlantic, from the Hawaiian islands to Puerto Rico, from the coast of California to the coast of the Carolinas, from Costa Rica to Florida. Several poems focus on Pawleys Island, South Carolina, my home surf. The river poems stretch from the Colorado to the Nile and Kebar rivers. The poems in this volume are about the ever-speaking seas and rivers. The seas and rivers are ever-living because they are always moving. I hope the reader can be moved by these poems to feel the energy of beauty therein and to sense the interior essence in each poetic scene.

The poems in this book are largely presented in pairs on facing pages—paired either by a common site or a common theme. Each panel of poems should be read together to enjoy the full effect. Some of the poems in this volume appeared in a chapbook entitled *Seascapes*, published by Finishing Line Press. I had the honor of seeing it nominated for the Pushcart Award. My thanks to Leah and Kevin Maines for this nomination.

Seascapes

1. this is my ink

Prologue Poem

The paper I inscribe, a transfigured pine,
is flatter now but no less tree to speak. Resin runs down my quill. Wings fly
across my page flashing shadows of some distant sun.
Or is it cuttlefish squirting jetblack fluid?
I am swimming for words when caught in a squalled sunrise.
A torrent flush treads the beach, bends fronds,
marches from the nor'east angry at nothing I know.
I can't see the light stars birthed four billion years ago. There's half
a million left to break. But I see the wind when it begins to sing.
And this is my ink.

I grab some sun and smear it across the face.
Tall light is better. Mixed color. Limbs limn a dream I've seen. Long after
I've hugged the night, I wake to watergreen trees stretching.
Or are they behemoths etched on caves?
I am tunneling for signs when trapped in an ancient earthquake.
A tsunami erupts over the cliffs, breaks Atlantis,
plunges a civilization into obfuscation.
I can't see the waves some faults spit thousands of years ago. There's half
a million left to break. But I see the wind when it begins to sing.
And this is my ink.

Dark clouds glorify the sun. They are fluid pilgrims
launching flights I've never winged. Singing is the fix to sorrow. Tomorrow
I'll get blown over in the storm surge, tumbled in bad waves.
Or is it that I will turn rain again?
I'm worming through libraries lost to ghosts and storms
trying to resurrect dead tomes from flattened pages
when another hurricane comes named Anastasia.
I can't see the whirl Africa pumped thousands of hours ago. There's half
a million left to break. But I see the wind when it begins to sing.
And this is my ink.

2a. twin epiphanies

North shore, Kauai, Hanalei Bay

twin epiphanies move me to mountaintop awe—
one that surges in liquid peaks of cloud breaks
and crashes of white thunder in swift plunder
terribleness turning quickly serene—spilling on reefs
into aqua green and translucent marine,
out of which another rises with palm-high peaks,
Na Pali majesty immersed in cloudy mists of gods
and lore of inspired Tahitians who crossed storms
in catamarans to these Hawaiian islands
blessed with supernatural mana, surf, and sun—
making me wonder if Hebrews were the only chosen
and if paradise was ever lost at all

2b. wet wild wind

North shore, Kauai, Hanalei Bay

our ears see before our eyes
as we mount a seacliff in northern Kauai
        wet wild wind in our faces
I scan long lines of distant waves undulating toward shore
in sets of four or five like fingers of some invisible hand
moving sideways just beneath the water's blue surface
        silent as darkness where nothing has voice.
I notice the fingers gradually knuckling up into bowed shapes
        while hearing closer waves drumming their end;
suddenly the fingers transfigure into liquid leviathans
        bellowing, hissing, moaning, roaring,
as the waves mount up into evanescent griffins—
stallions charging with spindrift manes, lurching behemoths
        crashing outer reefs, spewing white-high plumes.
        I have no speech! as I gape
at their mammoth faces breaking open, peeling, closing,
throwing down their vicious power on the rocks
like snowy leopards running in from the chase—
the kill, the spill of bestial music:
        poured out primordial booms accompanied by
        the fastest snare rolls I've ever heard—
        percussion peeking wild then thinning smooth
        like sizzler cymbals, morrocan shakers,
        brush strokes on taut antelope skin
        played by some invisible hands.

3a. seaside drum circle

east coast, Kauai

congas conk, cowbells clang, cymbals ting,
tap tap tap, stroke stroke stroke
bongos ping, rimshot rips, tomtoms flare
bang bang bang, blam blam blam
tablas thud, bassdrum booms, tamberines chink
boom boom boom, click click click
punctuated by breaking surf: crash, surge, sizzle.
the circle feels the primal pulse
percuss, percuss in syncopated thrust
as if it were a cylinder for the primeval voice—
bass booms depths (throbbing hearts)
congas climb into spirits that prance
                    animal-like, howl and hoot, jump and shout
click tongue and throat—as jungle and ocean mingle
in oval primeval rushing mix of sound all around
paradiddle paradiddle, flamcue flamcue
rrrrrrrrrrrrrrooooooooooooooolllllllllllllllllllll
ring ring ring crash; ping ping ping splash
slam tap slam tap slam tap. plash plash plash
five-stroke roll, seven-stroke roll, click click click
quick on every drum with flailing sticks and hands
connecting each drummer to the vibe of being
less than a beat away from Eden

3b. sacred motion

East coast, Kauai

unmanned ocean curls Kauai
        rides its lovers out to sea
and hurls them back again
        on roaring aqua surf.
the raw sacred motion
        of savage holy union
primes procreation seen—
        sea gives birth to surf and sands
ocean erupts a naked island
        sprouting glistening palms
and waterfalls running
        to wet their wild nativity.
its mystic sway juices islanders
        with rains that come and go
from punched potent clouds
        covering Kilohana peak
where that voice still speaks
        and sings in Wailua's falls
flowing down Na Pali's cliffs
        rambling on Waimea's trails.

I swear I've heard this poem before
but can't discern its sacred lore.

4a. riding giants in Hawaii

the ancient Hawaiians called it *lele wa'a* (canoe leaping):
seven men thrust a big canoe into the ocean
and six paddlers got up enough speed to catch a ground swell
while the seventh man, holding his board, leaped off the boat
onto a big wave and got a gorgeously long liquid ride

modern watermen call it tow-in surfing:
a jet skier towing a surfer speeds breakneck
into a wave as it's moving, mounting, surging high
and thrusts a foot-strapped surfer into the peak
of a twenty-footer or bigger—the taller, the thicker

in winter at Maui these waves get even larger—
the few watermen who charge into these waves
keep the Hawaiian spirit alive by chanting to the wind,
channeling Akua-God and tuning their bodies, spirits, and minds
to the cycles and rhythms of the swells in the Kona and Trades

the night before they surf Jaws, they listen to pounding breaks
and their pounding hearts; in the morning when they rise
they stand on shore and feel the ground tremble underfoot
as they watch the open ocean swell reach a shallow reef
and leap into a beauty of a beast they will dare to ride

some will wipe out in gnarly waves that sound
and look as big as Niagara falls—when the lip crashes
on a surfer's head and sucks his body over the top
and megatons of ocean pound concusive
pushing his body to dark depths never been before

others will get the ride of their lives
when in one momentous movement all the water
gets sucked up the face (like at Pipeline)
and it sets up perfectly: a slow, gigantic barrel
so powerfully dangerous, so beautifully magnificent—

surfing the biggest moving mountain on this ocean planet
is an adrenaline rush like no other granted, an incredible release,
a freedom to be one for one moment with the living Creator
as the surfer weaves his way down the mammoth face
of a wave as big as life and so much greater than self

4b. *He'e nalu*—Hawaiian surfer

out into the sea he paddles his olo against *paploken*
he waits and watches *lalaholaha*
way out he scans *he 'ale koa lolua noka moana*
he notes the sea's celerity, each crest and trough
as waves get closer he studies *homua nalu* and *'opi nalu*
the huge nalu puki curling behind him with white foam
his heart jumps! *nalpuki* comes—but he hesitates,
he's looking for a sweet *huia*
he passes up *halu 'ata* and *nalu nalu*
until finally he sees a perfect *kua nalu*
he paddles, *pae*, and *he'e nalu—halu kua loloa*

translation:
out into the sea he paddles his long board against breaking surf
he waits and watches the rising swell
way out he scans the long backed waves of the open sea
he notes the sea's clerity, each crest and trough
as the waves get closer he studies the breaker's base, the wave's bend
the huge swells curling behind him with white foam
his heart jumps! a big wave comes, but he hesitates—
he's looking for a sweet wave to surf
he passes up rough waves and waves that don't break
until finally he sees a perfect wave just about to break
he paddles, catches it, and surfs it—a good long ride

5a. watching my son surf

Wilderness, northwest coast, Puerto Rico

Earth rises to meet this morning's glow,
Spirit souls the sea, breathes into waves, wind climbs,
billows, heaves brute bends, buckle, gnarl, cave,
while beachcombers trim, brim, bend, curl, hurl
in the wave of, crest of, flung fetch of welter,
whether borreal, austral, euroclydion, or western—
the four winds of zoatic pneuma verve, gush
zephyrs, sprout bulbous, spill unctuous, cleave
reefs, island man, smashing cliffs, rock
and those who mean to surf the meanest break.
Most have to take the gentler smoother roll,
the sweeter stuff of waves, the lighter
and smaller peels, not breaking them to coral—
while you, my son, brave the rising leviathans
with rip, spin, cut, swirl, spray, and smile.

For Peter

5b. looking at my son surf

North Inlet, Pawleys Island, South Carolina

fishless and thick with sea
dark waves storm-wintered
stroke the shore with blackness
and push every soul away
except a few blackgarbed surfers
and one old man pushing a nor'easter

when the moon is long and sun thin
we forget the smell of sun and taste of wind

this flaw ends as suddenly as the seahawk snatch
as quickly as the next bareback catch of wave
glistening with glory in the curl and froth—
these whiteheaded waves are the breaking of age
good for the young to ride and shout
pleasant for the old to watch and contemplate

when the sun is long and moon thin
we remember the smell of darkness and taste of wind

For Peter

6a. pristine waves

Playa Guiones, Nosara, Costa Rica

Nosara, with promontory beaches
        and offshore breezes on swelling sea
azure, clear, and primed, a soulsurfer's dream
        (can't believe it!) that you gave me
longstrong rides on pristine waves—
        (how sweet!) the shape, the peak, the feel
of dropping in before the peeling break
        of sliding along a headhigh crest,
a mounting moving liquid face,
        of tucking under the windwhipped curl
as it began to bend (and thought would fall),
        but the wall held stiff by offshore gust
as I thrust into its hallowedness
        and entered a blessed sphere
where there's nothing but wind-and-sea,
        and I, an awed intruder (o spirit!),
who then slid out into foaming froth
        where a rainbow spray appeared
as miraculous as the wave (I caught it!)

6b. longest ride

Playa Guiones, Nosara, Costa Rica

I see what I have come to see so many days
at Playa Guiones: perfect surf in offshore breeze
under a covering of sunlight as *twanis* as life.
My confidence has risen to another height:
I believe I can take off higher in the crest
and make the drop without a fall.
Four in row—I can't believe it!
And then I paddle to wait the deepest sets.

A beauty is coming. I hesitate for a second,
thinking the Tico down the line will get it,
but I realize he's letting it pass for me.
I paddle hard, looking over my left shoulder
at the wave forming gorgeously. I take it
at its peak and make the drop by leaning back
on my board and then immediately forward
as I'm launched across the face of a gracious wave
that stays held up by the offshore zephyr
for longer than any I remember—

as I glide along eyeing this headhigh hyaline
I realize I'm face to face with miracle in motion,
as close to the quick of creation as I may ever be;
my heart is beating out my mouth
my mind is screaming, "this is my longest ride ever!"—
this wave that is long and sleek, strong and steady,
a beauty of a beast that moves me all the way to shore,
where I dismount my board and sit in awe,
trying to recapture as quick as I could
the sweetest, luckiest, longest wave I've ever surfed.

7a. between sea and cemetery

the cemetery at Playa Guiones, Nosara, Costa Rica

he sits under the archway
between sea and cemetery—
behind are rows of silent mounds
crowned with coral crosses
facing Hersperian hopes

outside past pounding breakers
a crowd of surfers sit deep, scan west,
squinting at the sun dropping into sea
like a wafer dipped in wine

he watches them bobbing up and down
in swelling mounds, their longboards
arching up like the headstones
behind him catching falling rays

while they all wait, passing waves
lilly up, shovel down, and break
into hundreds of thundered shreds—
and then they see, as he sees, a swell
swallowing the horizon, speeding their way
a decision quickens to leave land
and paddle deep into the almighty—

quick drop, heart stop, crouching
at the feet of the immanent Mover
who allows one epiphanic ride
down an uncertain line of liquid power
until it froths, hisses, thins, and hushes

7b. quick life

North end of Playa Guiones, Nosara, Costa Rica

I catch breath, dive underneath summersaulting break,
surface, bite another wave mount, reel, peel:
out of eternal circular flatness it mounds up
in multiple moving faces, walls up, glistens diaphanous,
bends fistulous, breaks, buckles, falls in percussive rushes.

Looking back I see tumbled sun burst white, turn thin light,
sizzle out, as each wave—quick life—is sucked back to sea.

When ocean reveals itself in flash of opened face,
the cast becomes a voice pitched as apocalypse—
a voice I first heard when the ocean began
hurling revelations so potent I was felled to my knees,
forced to measure my liquesence, the compass of my fetch.

Yet it's so hard to say the mystery I've heard, for as quick
as it's revealed, the sea scrolls itself into a roll I can't read.

Whenever I hear clouds coming and horses running on water,
I paddle into a herd of waves and let one after another pass
until there's one that bends its neck and gallops me to shore.
I know that's why I return again and again like waves—
I have hopes of unraveling lips as I catch a peeling break.

8a. caught up in the catch

fishing village near Cape Coast, Ghana

the young men muscled their way against the breakers
six in each dugout canoe stroked in unison and sang
until about 100 yards out they stopped and dropped
a 100 foot-wide dragnet, spread the seine in the shining sea,
then paddled back to shore with the two end lines—
while two swimmers stayed out to keep the net taut
the other 10 divided themselves between the two lines
and began a long arduous pull of net to shore.

as they pulled on the long ropes, they chanted and sang:
"give us fish, o Lord," huh-huh; "give us fish, today" huh-huh
"give us fish, o Lord" pull-pull; "give us fish today" pull-pull.
older villagers wrapped the lines around bending palms
that wore the grooves of a thousand previous catches
as they watched the young men cross the lines in an X
to trap the fish they'd been dragging toward the beach.

it looked as if the fetch was nearly within their reach
when the silver fish began flashing and popping up wildly,
the seabirds hovered on tottering wings just above them.
women appeared with straw baskets balanced on their heads,
children romped with glee in the foaming shallows,
while Eric and I were allowed to join in the beautiful pull
with the native villagers caught up in the catch!

8b. seaside soccer

fishing village near Cape Coast, Ghana

as the sun and sea surge and splash
men kick the soccer ball on the sandpacked beach—
back and forth their laughter lights the game
as pass after pass thuds to shots between the posts,
some that are stopped and some that are goals
but since no one keeps score, it doesn't matter.
what counts is fun for men who haven't lost what's young—
on and on they play, making labored runs and passes,
everyone on offense and everyone on defense:
"good ball" one shouts; "get back" another yells;
"nice shot" is praise raised from both sides of the shells.

there's something about the touch and roll of a soccer ball
that never gets old—a flick of a kick renews!
how sweet the ball's flight, like seagulls on the wing,
when it takes off and lands near a teammate's foot.
how cool the quick give-and-go, the one-timer,
the deft header, the nut-megger, the shot on goal.
if the muscles didn't ache and lungs gasp for air,
the ball could keep moving as long as day.
but even though the game must come to an end
and the beachside be emptied of all that fun,
the ocean keeps kicking up foam, making run after run.

9a. looking for a long right

La Jolla Shores, San Diego, California

a long right
a steep right
a hollow right
a memorable right
never interrupted by fall
a long right
a good right
a smooth right
an eternal right
that is what I look for
in the crooked
most of the time
I can't find it
but once in a while it's there
peaceful like uncalculated air
just floating between hemispheres
waiting for me to catch it
hanging there to fetch it
and when I get it, it gets me
there is nothing as good
nothing as free
not anyone has hallowed out
such a sacred groove
this is not to say I'm good
only occasionally lucky

9b. waves' faces

La Jolla Shores, San Diego, California

these waves have come from where I've never been
I know them only in their end
these bending tumblers, sleek divers, plunging headers
who spirit the *skene* one majestic minute
then just as quickly ghost away.
what puissance primed, pumped, and pushed them
into performance is never told by their faces
which we glide across leaving impermanent traces
of having caught them in their glory

10a. what the sea sees

Cape Cod National Seashore

Absorbing sunbreak and moonfall longer than bones,
earth's eyeball, half the globe filming
looks upward, not at us, peering at galaxies of God,
            while this turf has sucked the best and mean
and is the heavier for having taken down.

Not the ocean that survives with soul,
    it has a way of breathing.
Nothing I can say could make it swell—
dwarfed by its majesty I am dumb
but not deaf—the seawinds are my prophets.

Empires peak and crash—Babylon, Greece, Rome,
England, and other proud predicted powers—
but the sea sees none of them,
nor does the seawinged seahawk hovering wind,
            scanning waves, eyes fixed on ocean
until catching a phosphorescent flash of bluefish
            falls quick as light with open talons.

They will be this again and again
            the sea the sun the hawk the wind
long after everything human into humus has fallen.

10b. this moment

Cape Cod, Massachusetts

bluefish running fast
the gulls chasing minnows tell
fishermen fling their poles in hope of catch
while translucent crosscurrent waves crash
in a wash of white and curl.
          as for me this moment
I'd rather still and hear
the sound between waves
the sense between thoughts
the distance between lovers
as a sunny day turns suddenly gray

11a. the voice

Delray Beach, Florida

when a groundswell rolls in, bellowing,
billowing, curling, trimming, feathering
percussing arpeggio across this archipelago
the sea becomes my kithara and muse.
I immerse myself to fetch that voice
I first heard between cadence and crash—
the voice that spills from lips of waves
in the timbre of variegated aeolian peaks
cresting to crescendo falling in moreno;
somewhere in there between the breaks
I hear the oracle that makes life sense—
seagull caw, seahawk silent glide, pelican dive
into an ocean more majestic than awe.
rise. wind. wave. spirit. verve. I call
God who is coming God who has come,
the end is nothing more than what has been:
wind singing sea, sea surging bends and breaks—
in long strong stress waves musicate

11b. the voice again

Delray Beach, Florida

in long strong stress waves musicate—
wind singing sea, sea surging bends and breaks,
the end is nothing more than what has been:
        God who is coming, God who has come.
rise. wind. wave. spirit. verve. I call
        into an ocean more majestic than awe,
seagull call, seahawk silent glide, pelican dive;
        I hear the oracle that makes life sense
somewhere in there between the breaks
        cresting to crescendo falling in moreno
in the timbre of variegated Aeolian peaks,
        the voice that spills from lips of waves
I first heard between cadence and crash.
        I immerse myself to fetch that voice
percussing arpeggio across this archipelago
        billowing, curling, trimming, feathering
when a groundswell rolls in bellowing.

12a. wave watchers

Folly Beach, Charleston, South Carolina

the unsettled breezes master you
          west wind: stiff small waves. spray.
east: choppy mushy sections closing quickly
          northeast: firm rugged potent cliffs
southwest: with a swell, prime and heady.
          by wind and sun your color shifts
more subtle than skyshift
          afterstormblack, bottomblack, sharkblack
with yellowfoam turning brown
          greenbrown in armies of waves
one after another breaking in bluefroth
          into so many greens, hundreds of them
they are a roving jungle—
          verdant greens holding sunrays
summercool bluegreens inviting surf
          layered greens in euphotic shadows
the color switch of soundswish
          from murkiness to virescence
the mellowing of duskgreen
          from emerald to reseda
and all the bluegreen inbetweens
          hazel, jade, aquamarine
but nothing is more potent than silver
          quicksilver running down the waves
sleekgray in rainfall pitch and pull
          each drop making its moment
smoothing out wavemounds
          a desert of water mounting and falling
all else is graylost
          the clouds, the sea, the sky, and surf

12b. surfers

Folly Beach, Charleston, South Carolina

the sea is glass, a pond to skate on
a mirror for the sky's changing faces.
young tanned men come and go to shore
with waxed boards and fluid memories
but tide after watched tide drops their mood
like the half-lit moon in the west
but so does the pressure
            the ground slowly swells beneath the sea
bumping up substantial successive ridges
a southwestern holds them firm and strong
as they move along, rising higher and thicker
until they peak and trim a hundred yards long
each wave peeling off, dropping, pearling
as if some invisible finger slid down an ivory keyboard
            but the sound is not piano—it's percussion
tight snare roll, zildjian crash, morocco sizzle
as the surf breaks and stallions toward shore
past darting mullet and skimpering sandpipers
to the ankles of these bronzed islanders
bound to the sea and the board that takes them
beyond the chop, breakers, and roll
            where they watch the culmination
of arduous African migration
storm-swelled over far fetches
wall after liquid wall moves toward shore
as the surfers take off in fierce anticipation
of the thrill of standing under that curl
that can thrust or crush the interloper
who dares to call himself surfer

13a. sleek quick runs

Isle of Palms, South Carolina

a dreamed-of morning
for riding slowforming rollers near the pier
for taking sleek quick runs
                                        and soft salt falls
for diving into waves
                                        as if I were seagull

my only companions—looping dolphins and languid sun—
didn't scan how board/feet/wave/run
but it doesn't matter for they know no wave ever lasts

and I don't mind it passing
            like the last best set
for another is bound to form on my horizon

13b. sweet smooth sunned froth

Isle of Palms, South Carolina

jumps flash dash tropical dark
                    quick thick glory breaking
dolphins splurge spin
                              dive plash
pelicans
fall
from
sky
like
rain
while southwest spirit lifts waves
sustains
a surfer
          slicing sideways
                              down steepsleek wall
of white chasinghimlikesnowslide
weaves in and out
                    of furious surf
mounts up—brute stallion—takes off
cuts spins swirls
                    landing in trough
                              of sweet smooth sunned froth

14a. twilight surf

Frisco Beach, Cape Hatteras, North Carolina

dusk glows with a fiercer light than dawn—
it is the fantastic leaving of souls
it is the glory going, then gone
as when cathedral candles are snuffed
and smell strange in a dark room

first faint above thin pink wisps
the moon ascending heavy surf now faces
straight across a spit of swaying seaoats,
the sun burying itself into earth
and bloodying the western scape

the crescent star has the glory of its fallen twin
and lights the last two surfers taking turns
mounting and descending windwhipped peaks
until they tire and retreat to sand
where nocturnal glow claims dominion
as it rises higher on seasaw's end
tilting upward on seagull's wing

14b. gusts off the Outerbanks

Outerbanks, North Carolina

northeast gusts whirl off the Outerbanks
pumping line after seismic line of aqua waves
to our South Carolina coast glistening
in the early risen sun
winter is done—
May has come: the sea smells so, the sky,
the magnolia blossoms breathing open,
the confederate jasmine climbing into my nose

God knows I've sprung alive into life
as I paddle out past the white breakers
peeling from left to right, as I deep the sea
and see waves rising
on the horizon—
Duck diving, clinging to my wood, spitting sea water,
I'm thrilled to catch some super slick rides
down some long lefts. I'm always amazed I ride a wave
and wonder if God gives fins for an old soul to glide

I wish I could do this as long as the sun and sea
but I have only so many Mays to spring me,
more delicious as they pass, like drinking a cold
draught of apple juice
after the grass is mown—
the quick coldness plummeting from tongue
to blood, liberating every thought for a moment,
so that for the time being it just feels so cool
to be a human being, not a human doing

I've been so thirsty for a drink of spring!

15a. rolled waves

Pawleys Island Pier, South Carolina

sunless
sea and sky melt into each other's lines
like quicksilver, mercurial, sleeksmooth
in glistening grays slipping cool over the horizon
a comfortable dark, serene and unoppressive
over the wingspreadglide of egrets
and rolled waves bumping up like dolphinbacks
in the unscrolled moist oceanmorning mist
settles in like pelican flock
hovering landing floating bobbing biding
in the graywash, capecodish wetness
argent at surf's break, otherwise as solemn
and silent as the surfers' wake

I drink sundawn sea, mouth it moist,
smell lightyears bouncing off the breaks
(supernovae breaking speed)
mingled with fishswim old as God-thought
young as spindrift windkicked—
ah, birdwind, puffs of ocean rinsing morning me
in silent flight eyewise cocked toward surf-face
a string of seabirds streak the peeling line gawking
at sunbroken waves unhiding hundreds of fish in seaspill—
watch: waves, fins, wings all silverbacked whitebellied
dive headfirst in rush thrush of splash, plumage, and gills
quick keel and reappear as bobs in ocean yawn
surfing the moving moment of sea-spawn

15b. dawn intruder

Pawleys Island Pier, South Carolina

the ocean gray in the morning
usually catches some leftover light
from the moon
and there's always breaking
here and there some white churn which I slide down at eyes' height
beneath my feet
jacks dart blues dodge kings plunge
as I their surf intrude
paddling back I spot a mullet host
a gray ghost hovering on the green
popping jumping sliding whirling
the corraled won't leave their kind
fearing together is better
than escaping on their own.
slowly as the sun gallows in the hung mist
the commune is martyred
by invisible insidiousness—the jaws of ancient law
while I lay thin on my board
pretending to be invincible, watching the shade drift
now slimmer
than the horizon

16a. the beach is his

Pawleys Island, South Carolina

the beach is his. he makes it. the darting minnows
in surge, suck, sally. the sandpipers scurrying
between swooshes. the dallies with clawing crabs.
the pelicans bobbing on the sea like sun.
the swim, the search in crushed waves for the stick I pitched.
the fetch, prance, strut—like a majorette, he waves the stick
as high in the air as he can get it.
he is good so good. it is his universe.
those who stroll by sense, catch, smile, and share the glow
as we kick our way through the shallows
north wardheaded—I with board in hand and he with stick in jaw—
and slosh our way to the northern spit
where I begin to surf nor'eastern breaks and slide winddown
southbound breaking lefts, all the while trailed
by my companion who watches my catches and follows my drift—
excited by every ride, he runs along, my terrestial shadow.
and even if I mingle with a swarm of other blackgarbed surfers
he stays fixed on me until I ride the last wave to shore
where I am met in the shallows by the sweetest soul
with dance, swagger, primal joy, contagious happiness.
he wants more. so much more. never to leave the surging sea—
to chase dogs, rays, and falcons, to fetch, catch anything called life
but I exhausted soaked and spent, coax him toward the exit,
where we pass many a local who don't known my name
nor I theirs, but they call out anyway: "Hey, Charlie! how's the surf?"

for my golden retriever, Charlie

16b. dogangel

living on water and air and my love
I thought you'd make it to the warm days—
how you craved the sun as your body thinned
you still flared your nostrils to the wind
but couldn't chase. there was no more prance
left in you, though you wanted to please.

the last good day together we shared the beach
and winter sun with two families of dolphins
no more than a paddle away. they lit the ocean,
leaped, flipped, danced, dallied, pranced, played.
I know, Charlie, I know how you wanted to join—
you waded the frigid surf but couldn't swim.

the last grim days dragged slow as old January
and I spoke nothing significant and couldn't change
the end, as we watched one cold sunset after another
die. and I clung to keep the spirit of us alive
but I couldn't keep you from going to ghost—
I read it in your desperately sweet brown eyes.

the moment you left I went weeping to the drenched sea.
I passed some children throwing bread and laughing
as a swarm of cawing seagulls circled overhead.
then they shouted with delight into the cold mist:
"look, dolphins!" and I saw the twins streaming silver,
sea's angels, as sure of where they headed as eternity

for my golden retriever, Charlie

17a. mounting moving waters

Pawleys Island, South Carolina

the ocean sound is round. no separate sound of ocean.
        no wave of its own unfolding. up and down the coast
they'd been invoking an epiphany of wind on sea.

        how stoked after a long drought of catching next to nothing
to see it come—pumped, curved, conched, stretched out,
        peeling under dark clouds heavy air surging from the south—

a gaggle of waves, whitetopped, lining up, and pearling.
        paddling till our arms ached, backs tightened, legs cramped
eyes squinting in sunbursts through colorshapes running

        thickly, ghosting water, making all the white to grave rise.
froth, hoot, holler. Waves! who knows of tomorrow—
        they may thin in west winds. they may calm halcyon at dusk.

but this day is goodGodcreated and we are graced to take these breaks.
        the paddle. push. the jump. thrust. the weave. cut. the curve. slice.
the ride. glide—down long glacis, silent before crush, thick and sweet

        as the boardturn swish, I and wave. wave and I in one rush
of naturalness. of no telling of the sea from me, as I charge its break
        and wake and am thrust into sudden sacred hollowness

and come out flushed. flashed. having grasped the surge of, the pulse of
        the primal ocean winging wet wild flinging soaked piles
of mounting moving waters making breaking taking me along and down.

17b. take me down

Pawleys Island, South Carolina

silversea turns mauve in greydawn
            flat as horizon flat as sky
                        as I lay thin on my board and wait.
I cannot see but know the sun
            behind a veil of cloudsmear
                        there is halfyellow in the air
                        darkyellow in the waves
            as they curl peel drop disappear
            into ocean unscrolled across this stretch of earth
unsaying while waiting for some significance,
undisturbed except for plump pelicans diving thin
            and dolphins rocketing the surface
            exposed black to sun and rare to earth
                        splashing flat and loud and down and gone
            into the deepgreen goinggray undertowed
as suddenthunderheads press the surface
            pushing a wilderness of waves my way
ghosting darkhooded bentover and brave
            through a million spears plunging individually
into water (more water than thirsty God)—
            all is wet all is water all is soaked
the sky the sea the air and me—
            then just as suddenly the skies depart
and I spot a wave swelling
            bluebodied bareheaded resurrected
from its grave of flattened gray.
            I know that I must take it on
                        or it will take me down.

18a. earthrise sun

Pawleys Island, South Carolina

I caught the earthrise sun this morning
in a slit between two sheaths of clouds
one hanging on the water like a lover
the other hanging from the sky like a thief.
As the sun passed through these, it lingered
just long enough in between to mean something.
I snatched this sign and ran it to the sea
where I surfed the day by waves by storm,
as ghosts of water fell on breaks and peaks
turning them velvet, soft, supple, sheen.

18b. perfect day

Pawleys Island, South Carolina

sunny skies. offshore wind. storm kicking waves
a hundred miles out. blessed surf—sublimely shaped

breaking right and left in a serene northwest.
at first I have them to myself. then others come,

mostly friends. so I don't mind sharing surge,
slide, glide, splurge. the wave jumping high, tubing,

peeling down the line, as I ride long lefts from peir
to the groin. and rights all the wave back again.

others do the same as I paddle back out. some hoot.
some holler. mostly the ocean sings. it soothes,

it moves, as spirit sustains. wind and sea and sun
and man in confluence: evidence that God is good.

19a. I return like morning to the sea

Pawleys Island, South Carolina

The summer air is crisp on Pawleys Island
from an offshore wind holding up waves
giving them sleek faces with hoary heads
on the swollen Atlantic, rolling, unscrolling
in apocalyptic blue at sunbreak in birthed light.
As beachcombers rise I ride some peeling
breaks, while my golden retriever gazes, waits,
then wanders off in search of minnows
sallied into shallows, sucked back in undertow.

As I paddled out I admire pelicans wing horizontal
to the sea, surfing the air just before the peeling waves:
one turns toward the sun, rises on wing span,
dives with tucked pinions into a swirling school,
emerges with a mullet in its gullet, lifts its throat
to the heavens, and swallows the wriggling bread.

As I lay on my board scanning the billows
rising up and rolling, a pod of grey dolphins butterflies
across the vista opposite the pelicans.
They circle, leap, flap fins and dive, as they call their own
to join the net around a heap of swelling blues.

Further out I am startled by a stingray big as day
rocketing the water with angelwings and devilhorns
sprouting from its head and skin as smooth
as dolphin, gray as shark, terrifying as imagination.

In all of this the sun is silent, pelicans are silent,
dolphins are silent, and so are the blues and ray.
I am silent, my dog is silent, and so is the horizon.
Only the breaking waves break the silence.

The silent God has watched night, watched stars,
heard the sun rise and break open day like bread.
And that is why I return like morning to the sea,
whether the waves are not or good.

19b. sea-spawn

Pawleys Island, South Carolina

I drink sundawn sea, mouth it moist,
smell lightyears bouncing off the breaks
(supernovae breaking speed)
mingled with fishswim old as God-thought
young as spindrift windkicked—
ah, birdwind, puffs of ocean rinsing morning me

in silent flight eyewise cocked toward surf-face
a string of seabirds streak the peeling line gawking
at sun-broken waves unhiding hundreds of seafish in seaspill—
watch!: waves and fins and wings all silverbacked whitebellied
dive headfirst in rush thrush of splash and plumage and gills
quick keel and re-appear as bobs in ocean yawn

I'm surfing the moving moment of sea-spawn

20a. hummingbird in hurricane

Hurricane Charlie, August 14, 2004

We hurry inland from falling floods
swollen seas birthing outrageous rush
            in fast force of wind mounting waves
climbing up the back side and tumbling
over the front in a spill of white upon white
      in seasurge crush and push of dunes and air
            erasing the horizon smearing the line
      between firm terrain and watery main.

A mile inland there's no sun than what's believed—
as the slim trees bend shiver break
weeping willows uproot drooping
      elms unbranch and fly like pelicans
pines curve contort twist and vault
as we hear leaf-sizzle treesnap crash
            and the hurricane raining down wind.

During this assault I was startled to spot
            the hummingbird who lives in our woods
gripping a flailing magnolia branch
flapping in gusts like a lose haulyard—
and with wings whirling cyclone fast and furious
            helicoptering in the horrific hurricane attack
      long enough to sip some nectar from a cup
then speed like wind through bending pines.

20b. brute beast

Hurricane Katrina, August 2005

Unmothered brute beast bends nature
        bullies seas into heave, growl, ghoul
not descriminating whose marrow it sucks—
shores, homes, trees, and thinner structures, man—
as it dumps heaps of water deeper than despair
that there's no God of Noah near.

While smothered souls give up their ghosts
        to spirited places where Spirit roams,
others climb to attics and axe their way to air
and hovering angels rapturing their fear.
They are not, as desired, winged to refuge
but to where nothing is doing human well.

Here and there among the groping diaspora,
        saints appear as living light unearthing cheer,
beaming hope, absorbing pools of tears.
And this is what makes me think there's still
some deity left from the God who humaned us
and that his Spirit can inspire us to grasp
    that grace is given when faith is lost.

21a. September surf

September 4-14, 2005, when hurricane Ophelia was spinning off the South Carolina coast for days on end

As I stiffleg a sandy trail from marsh to ocean
 I hear what the waves appear to be
and can't wait to immerse my head in water
 warmer than the air. I'll push my legs to bend
one more session as I come to where sea lands
 and moves a man still strong enough to paddle
and aged enough to know I won't always
 have strength to break beyond the breaking surge.

But for this day I am good enough, as I am drawn
 by the cresting and curling sea exploding
into whiteness from dark nothing. I'm awed by swells
 mounting to shore with epiphanic faces.
It's amazing that the rude ocean lines up in the end:
 beachcomber after beachcomber rakes
shoals, beach, and brim in even strokes.

And all this because a hurricane churns the Atlantic our way,
 pushing northeastern waves for days on days—
in sweet swells pearling to the surfer's left
 blowing spindrifts in occasional offshore gusts,
or in strong rushes shoaling too swiftly to catch.

The day before the hurricane hits, I surf to the end
 of my strength, until the last glory of dusk,
as the clouds overhead clutch as much sheen as they can
 in an eerie glimmer brightening before it dims.

In the morning the outer bands circle our way,
 dropping sky into sea, pummeling ocean into sand;
by afternoon the typhoon has swallowed sun
 and risen leviathan in ocean lunging at land,
pounding the pier, crushing a few crazed surfers—

it's wild, it's wierd, it's the wind conquering earth
whenever it can. And it does it best with heaps of water
 so beastly beautiful, so awfully powerful,
so close to killing and kind to quicken water into waves.

21b. broken open ocean

Tropical Storm Faye, August 2008

broken open ocean,
such strong faces form on you
as you leap from the abyss, peel off,
and fall all over yourself—
that is when your waves are best

you break me with force louder than voice
of the mingled roar of wind and wave—
you suck all my strength away—
as I swim weak into your potent wake

broken open ocean,
savage sea with warrior waves
and power longer than thought,
stronger than human mind or might,
I break in humility, confess your majesty

your thrust forces me to my knees—
I cannot stand, I stagger in the wend,
bottomed out, I cannot blame or scold
that I am old and you are always younger

22a. "aniphany"

creatures here below
quiet as God go
and I to them a stranger
paddling wood in their wake
as they break sea before me
and we eye each other face to face:

the green sea turtle in Hanalei Bay with cranial growth
and yet another who was perfectly sleek and serene
the loggerhead in the Atlantic brim who looked as old as sea
the sluggish manatee whose dark form crossed my watery way
the bottlenosed dolphin in Carolina who surfaced for play
the pod of dolphin who surrounded me and my Californian cousin
the mustached sealion who surfed the same wave with me

they each broke thin secrecy and spoke
not of ocean depths festooned in darkness
        but of light that sprinkled me many an oceanless day

22b. dolphin dawn

Emerged from the silver sea
a hump of bestial beauty
levitating a moment between
aquatic and aerotic worlds
then with brimming face puggy and serene
pushed a glow into everywhere dark—
before taking a quick breath of light
and plunging into invisible silver.

Though the rest of the day was gray
I breathed lighter
thinking how close I got to God.

23a. ocean oaks

Ocean old, they sprawl, stretch, gnarl, wear the sea,
cling trellised to the dropping sky—
their heavy branches having shoved their way
into sunshine without man or beast having seen
any exertion or maneuvering underneath.

As we stroll under them, we're amazed how they tangle
with heaven, we marvel at the knobby canopy
that shades us, both generations before and beyond,
and we imagine who layed under their boughs
drooling spanish moss, catching summer breeze
with wind-twisted trunks spiraling skyward
then downward into bended crook and crawl—
so unlike the erect pines piercing into blue,
the oaks hang with us—they linger round
our homes and grow on us like longtime friends,
they become our hands with so many clinging fingers
grasping our longings for everlasting climbs—
this is their sacred glow, that they outlive us
yet never forsake us like some unearthly soul
seeking release from earth's heavy burdens.

And so we never believe that one could come to an end,
until our path brings us to a skeleton oak—
its tawny brown ashened, its angels turned to ghosts,
and its fallen wings dry and brittle
snapping underfoot. Yet still it somehow stands
with no sap sucked from heavy earth; it stands
heavy among the living. And I don't understand,
no I can't, why its roots got weary of seeking
and its boughs of stretching—or could it be
that earth tires, letting us all go one by one?

23b. sea acacia

there were times of singing but it has been way too long
since then, way too deep hide the vowels of joy
for me to well them up again. they were there once
I remember, I recall singing, I remember joy and the taste
but my tongue is soaked with saltwater, my heart soused with wine
my bones are shaking, my fingers tremble on broken rhyme
my pen moans like a broken vessel warped by slanted seawind

in the ancient waters I see long spirits rising and dying
invisible horses churning the waves, angels treading water
onto the broken shore where a sea acacia with sea limbs
crooked by gnarly winds holds terra firma only as long as . . . . .
you've outsung me, old man, but not the sea of winds.
the ocean always wins; it won't paean you or me
as we seagreen and our roots topple upsidedown

24a. I am sea

I am sea, so much sea,
wind-strong, sun-long, moon-swollen,
I fill myself with what I am.
I break but am never broken.
I swell in waves' potent rise
and fall upon my own liquescense.
I always calm after stormwindhowl—
I fall back on the sea I am.

I am sea, ungraspable sea.
Before there was any separation of land from me
I hushed darkness with thund'rous breakers,
imprisoned legions of leviathans,
seaMonsters, seaDragons, seaDenizens,
unbreathing deep beneath me.
Hades and Abyss plumb under my perception:
I can let them live or kill the myths.

I am sea, inconquerable sea.
No one can step a foot on me, light or heavy,
pound a stake into my main and make claim.
With no cause to war over me,
I see men surrender to my power. I am not an enemy,
though I've swallowed many to the dregs,
more have swallowed me and begged for what I cannot give.
I cannot breathe life into the dead.

I am sea, but not Almighty.
God's lunar palm pushes me so far but never more;
his fingers keep me from breaking beyond the brims.
I crave to break unbounded on every side,
go roundless, edgeless, unanchored, unformed.
But he stops me from rushing unbodied, unfettered,
and chokes my mighty water with suffocating powers,
from breaching every human boundary.

24b. Had I been chaos

Had I been chaos rising from mist, light cleaving
darkness, I could have seen your invisible hand make your mind
come alive with spinly pines, gnarly oaks, redwood cedars, poking
the tall azure sky with leafy heads, dropping their own peculiar seed.

I could have gleamed flesh of every kind, as you filled surging seas
with fecund fins, gills, legs, eyes, and swim. As you flashed
the skies with swarms of wings, beaks, talons, caws, and fly.
As you forested earth with crawling fur, claws, teeth, limbs, and
fetch. As you formed man with brain, braun, beauty, spirit, and
grasp. I would have touched. More than I imagine.

I wasn't there when you came. But others were. Fishermen.
Those who smelled the seawinds. They saw the invisible.
They clawed the air and found. You came breaking loaves
and minds. Their hearts poured. Their words gushed fullness.
I have drunk the more than I can tell. I am satiated and still.

25a. the breathing speaking sea

The sea is a breathing body,
its waves, like throbbing heart, beat
against the shore, billowing blood—
it lunges and expands like lungs
filled with wind from Spirit God—
my spirit succumbs to awe
as I silence myself before you,
extinguish terrestial thoughts.
I drink your marine muses
until my soul's suffused.
Speak me into everlastingness,
tell me I'm wave and wind curled.

I am your congregation listening
to you proclaim the Spirit's course
(in the wisdom of fluid Qoholeth)
from God to man and back again,
come to hear the spirited truth
as waves return to ocean
older than tall mountains,
stronger than snaking rivers,
longer than human history—
I come with open ear to hear
in fathoms deeper than mystery
what wind on waves has to say.

25b. listen to the sea

he mornings deathdark shadows
dips day into darkest night
buckets oceans of heavy water
sprinkles earth with precious rains
carves mountains, stirs winds,
reveals his thoughts to quiet beings

after one sun falls into the ocean
the night sun rises heaven's queen
with an entourage of circled stars
who make the heaven's music—
yes, there's a singing in heaping stars
(spoon mouthfuls of cymbals, drink timbrels!)

divine drones oscillate in orbits
percussing rhythmic waves on our drums
(tune them beyond our sphere);
though most have drowned the oracles
there are those who swim watery worlds
who've always sung pelagic poems

I paddle out, lay prone on the flat sea
(ear to the deep) in quiet uncertainty—
I await the epiphany emerging quick
in those who pierce the membrane,
spit darkness, squeal light, dive back
(don't be dumb, catch the sight)

26a. shadow catcher

as each day rises over the hill and flops into the sea
he thrills at what he grasps—he's so joyful it's painful
his eyes inhale vanishing visions before nightbreak
he breathes epiphanies and catches meaning in flight

the thin understand he wings to secret spaces
so sweet and wild God lives there for awhile
just long enough for the quick to click a look

when distress of darkness passes, he catches a breath of sun
when the wind begins to sing, he holds private dawn
when the sea surges to rhyme, he inks the pungent sound

he stores these images in his mind like bottles in a winery;
he relishes each one—the color, texture, taste, and feel.
uncorking is dangerously ephemeral, pouring is sweet,
swirling a mystery—is it wiser to treasure or better to drink?

in wisdom he leaves everylivingthing as it pristine is—
its essence he does not steal; its nature he can't control
he catches moments as shadows racing from the sun

he fetches the broken side (pain takes me there,
peeled off pride)
he glimpses invisible eyes
as he ciphers sacred spaces and snaps apertures

26b. spiritual soul

as the day dawns, stars fall from the sky,
clouds crawl off the sun, rays thin into my skin,
and I begin to plough the light before another night

I long to be a spiritual soul, not wait after-death life.

like a corry sherewater I live two worlds—air and water,
I spread my wings to harvest all the candlepower
the filtered rays can muster; I swim the seas for food

I long to be a spiritual soul, not wait eternal good.

far away nebulae, bright quasars, super novae
birth luminosity too bold and bright for me—
I'll gather sunlight before it falls into the sea

I long to be a spiritual soul, not wait eternity.

27a. ocean incantation

the ocean's incantation is tantric to my ear
magic mantra motion turns the wheel of prayer

the sea is breathing deeply and I'm inspiring
the celeritous cycle cleansing all desiring

as the body of the sea releases its living chi—
eternal energy flows kundalinic in me

let me not die my daily dreaded deaths
let me breathe the zephyrous breaths

ubiquitous voice echoing from shore to shore
there is more to hearing you than mystic lore

27b. the sea also rises

the sea also rises tide after tide
in refluent resurgence:
in sempiturnal seriation,
wave after sinuous wave
strikes sticcato on the shore—
there is more resurrection
in this ocean than I can imagine.

its fullness breathes and overruns
as its vast body rises
diurnal from its depths.
I feel the eternal recrudesce
and fill my lungs with breeze and song—
there is more transformation
from this ocean than I can contain.

28a. aqua planet

So much of this heavy earth is water,
so much of this water is heavy sea—
this aqua planet flows blue as sky,
green as grass across the living globe.
No one knows why it hurls and heaves
and why it abruptly stops at beaches' edge.
No one can count its myriad miracle waves
or fathom its ever-darkening depths.

Strong is sea, as long and strong as wind.
Life is sea, as breathing and living as God
who said, "let waters swarm with living creatures"
and inspired seas with multifarious features—
billow and white burst, bend and break,
rollers, beachcombers, pipeline tubulars
that take me in the surf of momentous break
as I'm thrust headlong into pelagic wake.

28b. ride the heave

along the jagged horizon as in a Serengeti migration
the wind shoves a herd of waves hurrying ahead of storm

gusting a gaggle of waves, a swarm of surf in torrid downpour
deserting the sea to a watery wilderness pitching cresting falling

the only white in all this world is wavecrash foam and froth
the clouds, sea, sky, surf smear. mingle. mix in a world awash.

wind is rain and rain wind. no sun to tell the time. only the tide.
in all this drenched gray the only lumen is surfbreak

and flash of mackerel silver on the quick underside
chased by tigersharks dark with hunger, while we ride

the heave break snap curl of the hurling seabend
juiced with cloudbursts and surfers clinging on

to the pumped primed lunging sea flung and flattened
flung and flattened in seabend break and snap

wet with hunger wet with cold wet with wild waves
we don't surrender until much too much beach appears

29a. edge of the sea*

I watch the soft sea fog blur the sea rocks' contours
as the sky and sea's gray mist mingle offshore,
and I hear the sea's voice in the surge of rising tide
creating a tumult of watersounds, swashings, swirlings—
a perpetual slapping against the rocky rim of land
with undertones of murmurings and whisperings,
suddenly obliterated by the water's torrential inpouring—
all because the bloated moon is aligned with the sun.
The springtide (*sprungen*) has impregnated the ocean
to brimming fullness with strong, long movement
of surges leaping and dancing over jutting rocks
in long cascades of foam spilling on the edges.

In the recurrent rhythms of tides and surf,
the long rhythms of planet sea on planet earth,
the marl has been sculptured in bays and cays
by sea forces pressing forward, receding, returning—
the sea's edge perpetually reclaimed by the rising tide
bringing food for flamingos, sanderlings, and gulls—
the ebb exposing the long prop roots of mangroves.
As land and sea interchange their lives, the coast
is constantly transformed from face to face—
and I imagine it once a lovely unpeopled place
where darkness ruled night, moon was the only light,
and days were as long as lonely beaches.

*This poem was inspired by Rachel Carson's *The Edge of the Sea.*

29b. visit to the seaside

suffering fastfood, tollways, cramped legs
he drove to the coast to catch some wind
to comb the beach for conch
which bagged back to the city compensate the ear
here and there
he meandered the shallow shoals
admiring tide carvings and sloping rippled canyons
stepping into pools of darting minnows
and rays trapped thin as sunlight
looking off aways he spotted dolphin
humping the horizon
and pelicans penetrating seaglass
invisible, like music, the wind picked up
and played the sea as if it were harp
each wave falling in rhythm to the hum

he stripped to the waist and plunged
sea-soaked, salt-rinsed, head-drenched in tumbling rollers
slammed into sand, a smattered shell

30a. mystical migration

South Carolina coast

it's early October in Carolina
when creatures metaphysic south
most in broods and pools:
pelicans, cormorants, egrets
arrowing blue heavens

spots, whitings, blues
chased by black cold and sharks.
my instincts tell me follow
but there's no way to morph
unless I quickly wing or fin

somehow crysalis uncocoons
from pupa darkness with wings
colored sunrise and surprise:
there is transfiguration—
God can change after all

leaving behind shed
blood and skin these miracles
fling into translucent cherubim—
metamorphosis in flight
gives us rise to sing!

as I worm along the beach
one by one they flit pass
magnificent every few minutes
following the coast religiously
on some supernatural route

I gaze at their salmon wings
painted with black auspice
praying to divine the sign
as each alone pilgrims
to a home it's never been
October is nearly over

I hear the weather falling
fear the failing sun
they're gone like souls
disappeared and sainted

but I remember a few weeks
ago watching their noiseless wings
move them quicker than waves
and I'm braved to imagine a place
even God would like to live

if they know where to fly
at summer's end shouldn't I
sense when paradise begins
and lift imago wings
to austral winds and rise?

yes! when the call comes
to uncocoon and unfurl
diaphanous wings thin as angels
flying nowhere near imagination
I will split, flare, and wend

30b. unscrolled voyage

mid-October in coastal South Carolina

flocks of monarchs flit pass, seeking southern sun—
how I thirst to become light and wing with them
out of sight of winter's too old, too cold eyes—
my mind unscrolls with these voyaging cherubim
to warm Mexican mountains, to Pacific groves.

how I'd love to journey with these angelic gypsies
who beat death by beating silent wings.
I read their flight in volumes of message—
each monarch a floating book, thin as papyrus
written in black ink with story older than Scripture,
bolder than Moses shouting from the bush.

I have somewhere to follow better than sadness
when I worm out of this body, turn chrysalis,
shed blood and skin, unravel wings to the winds,
free fly, free rise, unweighted, unabated
into more soar than transfigured dream

I am going where I've never been or seen,
to a joyous panegyric I taste with my spirit.
I will join the million myriads gathered in the air
suspended between this earth and heaven
in flocks of festal orange enjoying journey's end—
with the best of transmigration yet to begin.

we will come again to grace woods and meadows
to wing and whirl. our leaving means parousia is near—
as it is written on our paper pinions, we are circular
minions: death to us is life and life is not death,
as we give voice without ever making noise.

30c. invisible feel

tribute to the monarch butterfly

while I put wings on flat words and fly them
across sheets and sheets of thin paper,
every October they migrate farther than thought:
red ladybugs, death's head hawkmoths,
painted lady butterflies, libellula dragonflies,
and the glorious monarch butterflies
whose wings fling them to Mexican mountains
where they congregate with a million pilgrims,
making me believe there's solid heaven beyond every verb

as I sense their presence come, the presence goes,
an invisible feel I've come to know—
a finger of cool wind turns my head
to spot a monarch undulating near the sea,
light a rose, sip nectar, unceremoniously ascend—
though I know her invisible eyes don't glory
in the beauty of her magical majesty,
I wonder if she's aware, as she flings wings south
she's been marked to be my pioneer

31. Boxing Day tsunami (2004)

the ocean was drawing back into itself
like a god pulling in a deep breath

children frolicked on the revealed seafloor
jumping in small waterholes of the new foreshore
while their parents explored the uncovered terrain
a few locals came down to fetch some gasping fish
while others stood back warily

    having never seen the ocean rush backwards

perhaps it was the new moon's tug and pull

out to sea some scuba divers descended
        into their dive and were rocked
    by a strangely strong underwater roll
yet they ascended into calm and sun

a couple sunning on their sailboat deck
spotted one ripple like a long pipe speed by them
and pass underneath
    they studied it as it humped toward land
mounting ever bigger into a bloated seaserpent

    some Tai fishermen even deeper in the deep
felt a wave pass underneath them and rock their ship

a surfer sat on his board scanning the horizon
    searching for some oncoming swell
he saw flat sky flat sea and the line where they meet
until out of nowhere the sealine gobbled the sky—
he dropped to his stomach and paddled for his life

in Yala Sri Lanka and the coasts of the Indian ocean
elephants chained to palms snapped their chords
    and lugged children to higher ground
water buffalo, langur monkeys, leopards sensing terror
                broke to the mountains
as did the Jarawa, Onge, Sentilese, and Andamanese
    the natives who've gathered nature long

but not the tourists and some locals
        who continued to comb uncovered beaches
heads down looking around for shells and such—
not seeing the oncoming rush but hearing a drone
        growling like jet engine thrust
looked up and out to sea

as the horizon transmogrified
        into a dark blue leviathan mounting
        a black smoked seamonster
        with frothy head and mammoth face
        with rush faster than thought, higher than God
        a wave that did not curl or break after it built
        but pushed heaps of apollyon with watery fists

grabbing their children by their hands they ran
        as the torrent ate land beneath their feet
ripping babies from mother's grip, hurling bodies
into palms, suffocating children in foam,
chasing the swiftest sprinters into jungles,
sucking the strongest swimmers
        past floating corpses ripped back to sea

and this was just the first almighty crash
on that sunny sunday morning after Christmas

the second swelled like hoods of a giant cobra in the sky
charged more hellion than apollyon rushing shores
like Herod's dark army on Bethlehem's streets
stripping mothers of their children
in death worse than rape
spewing seawater everywhere people can't drink
        spewing corpses everywhere people can't fathom
the living swim through them, those clinging to palms
or hanging to balconies watch them pass—their lovers,
their mothers, their sons and daughters beyond
their grasp as the quick seasurge sucks as swiftly back

some swallow water because they have no power
others swallow sea to hasten death

half the people in half the debris fall to the earth
of broken bodies, mangled cars, hotels, and boats
the other half are raked back to sea like seaweed
returned the next few mornings as bloated oblations
to some god gone crazy or god gone dead

*

The man on the Sri Lanka beach stood there caught
between life and death and didn't know which as he saw
the seabeast mounting He heard it growling
when it pounced on him he was tumbled into watery
darkness into layers of deep waters unlit abysmal
obsidian waters swimming in pelagic depths
going deeper and darker This blackness was so dark
there were no shadows no gradation from black to grey

Obsequious this darkness wrapped around itself took
itself over demonized itself as darkness possessed
with itself It was very slow blackness the kind of blackness
that's going nowhere because there was nowhere to go
but deeper darkness There was no peeling away
no stripping down to something other than darkness
which fell heavy as chaos There used to be something other
than watery darkness but for now earth was drowning
and all that was in it He was tumbling in the darkness
of azoatic obsidian There was nothing called sky horizon
space or breath Earth trembled under the pressure
The subterranean shook and cracked the sea making waves
breaking into other waves across sealong fetches
waves mounting in the offing rising leviathan crashing mushing
reforming mounting cresting collapsing intermingling
with a million other waves colliding swirling going nowhere
in oceans of confusion in lull and lunge lunge and lull
water falling upon water with no shores to take
the fall Liquid cymbal clangs with liquid cymbal in dark
sound of it all Rush and roll Roll and rush on shoals

sandbars reefs Deep from caverns the waves leaped lunged
plunged spilled fell from dark pitch crash crush roar sizzle
The surge the slosh the rush crush crash between each
fetch and flush in long stretches of nothing but darkness
pushing darkness into blacker spaces Faceless mirrorless
unconscious water making itself seas drowning itself
in listlessness and yaw in plunge to deep in depths of gone
going deeper A strangle of water suffocating earth
A liquid ring as round as nimbus moon but no glow
only gloom in the dirge of surge upon surge flapping
fishless fetches of lonely stretches of horizonless seas
seizing seas A tumble of black rolling into black and back
again into nothing but wash wave lunge surge lull crash
flush churn This sea a monster heaving reeling in heavy

wetness in dark so fat nothing could wriggle
between the cracks Leviathan sits behemoth on paws
fanning its serpentine tail over what used to be fecund
lumined soil All is Waterwithoutlight Deepwithoutlife
A desert of sea everywhereGoingnowhere
for there was no horizon no separation of sea from sight
no beach no wind of light to open to break bleak bands
and hardly a survivor left.

A few crawled through the nightsea to see some spirit
smack damp black in half and an eyelid crack the dawn
The sultry shroud lifted and the single eye unveiled pealed
sky beamed seas The lit disk ember-orange surged hot from
burning styx exorcised murkiness swallowed shadows
between waves made cool waters rise and ghost from earth
It was a day for wind taking light and throwing it all
around between the shades and troughs for drawing
the long thin horizon line as circular as an eye
It was a day for epiphanies of color for the parousia
of the sun's soft skull rupturing the oval horizon flushing
it bloodshed red raw and strange more crimson than color
for slaying black leviathan of its lair and lore.

But on some of the islands there was not a soul to scan
the ocean sun in hue shift more subtle than skyshift
afterstormblack bottomblack sharkblack with yellowfoam
turning brown greenbrown in swarms of waves one after
another breaking in bluefroth into so many greens
hundreds of them more than the forest trees and plants
a roving jungle of verdant greens holding sunrays lit greens
in translucent beams springgreens summercool bluegreens
layered greens in euphotic shadows There was not a soul
to catch the colorswitch from murkiness to virescence
the mellowing of duskgreen from emerald to reseda
and all the in-betweens of hazel jade aquamarine.

*

Satan walked the shore and counted the dead
mostly children and women who couldn't outrun the flood

Jesus walked the sea and counted those who saved
themselves and those who just were saved:

the man who jumped from a wrecked train
cluttered with floating corpses
and found refuse on a nearby rooftop

the boy who gripped the luggage rack
until the water subsisded

the family
who grabbed
their hotel towels
climbed palms
and tied
themselves on
till dusk

a fisherman who
climbed a pole
with daughter
on his back
and two sons
in each arm
holding and holding
slipping and slipping
until the two fell
into the surge
and seemed to drown

later they were found half buried under sludge
and handed to him who cried and sighed,
"why did God choose to save my children
when he let so many others die?"

an Indian boy clinging to a treetop
who heard his mother scream
his name,"Ardiyansah!"
before she succumbed to sea

another boy, Chia-ni, flung onto a coconut tree
who wailed a day and night before he was taken down

a young Tai washed downstream
who saved himself by clutching riverbank roots
as the water kept surging overhead—
he struggled to surface several times
only to hear his mother scream,
"where are you? where are you, my son?"

another Tai boy who believed he breathed underwater
until he was flung to safety on the shore of a jungle

a Hong Kong couple clinging to a mattress
careening through the streaming living and dead

a new baby sleeping on a floating mattress

a six year old, Zoe Shiu, grasping a cushion

        a Swedish toddler tossed into sludge
        rescued by Americans and restored
        to his father's heart bereaved of love

the 26 orphans
whose thin peninsula
was being engulfed
by water cascading over the lagoon on one side
and pouring in from the estuary's mouth on the other
whose Christian leader, Daylan Sanders
quickened by Scripture
(*when the enemy comes in like a flood,*
the Lord's Spirit raises up a standard)
gathered them quickly into a boat
that he steered straight into the oncoming tsunami
        knowing their only hope
    was not to outrun the surge
but to get on top and ride it out like Noah's ark

    the children on a Thai shore
    who were hoisted to the back of an elephant
    that had been brought to the beach to entertain

the son of Sangreta, an Indian mother
who with three young sons and only two hands
shouted to her oldest, "Run, run, Dinakartan!"
but he fled into their hut where he was sure to drown
had not it been for their old yellow dog, Selvakumar
who urged him to the jungle and his mother's arms

    the man trapped three days and nights
    under the wreckage of his boat and house

the man buried under debris for two long weeks
    who lived on nothing but faith

Satan scoured the sea and counted the floating corpses
Jesus walked the waters and saw the few who rode it out

the Indonesian man, Rizal, who was found afloat
after three days of clinging to an uprooted tree

an Indonesian woman, Malawati, who was pulled from sea
after five days of riding a sago palm
whose bark and fruit she ate, as fish and sun did the same

a Sri Lankan fisherman, Mohammed Sarfudeen,
who clung to his capsized boat for three days and nights

the fishermen who survived eight fiercesome days
under ruthless sun on a drinkless sea

*

in the days after, if you could call them days,
mothers groped the shore
for bodies to appear
fathers wandered the debris
wondering if it's better to be the stench
or smell

others searched desperate
photos of the living and lists of the deceased
trying to match the two

uncertainty is excruciating
but is it greater than the agony of a mother
falling headlong when she discovers her child
drowned under a mound of sludge?
or the anguish of those whose children
slipped from their watery fingers?

all along the Sri Lankan coast
bodies were scattered like broken shells
emptied of their souls

Hindus burned corpses quickly hoping to kill memory
hoping fire is stronger than water
and water is not longer than love

a monk found a corner in an overcrowded Buddhist temple
to meditate and chant, but he couldn't transcend
his painful thoughts, "Siddartha has no answer for death,
only for suffering—yet not this. The sea is not illusion."

a priest in a makeshift morgue
struggling once again to find some words for the dead
and words for the living,
thought but did not say, "there's no theodicy here—
though some have seen miracles, God seems to hide
behind faces blurred and wrenched with agony,
from eyes raised to heaven,
from that bereft mother hunched there mumbling blame
and that father rummaging for his child
among a pile of bodies about to be bulldozed down a pit.
The earth, for all its sweetness and wonder,
is a dangerous place to live and a good place to leave."

a Sunni imam in an Indonesian mosque on friday morning
knowing he's supposed to tell the congregation
that punishment falls on those who do not follow
Allah's laws and have been seduced by Western thought,
forced himself to castigate those who lost their children
and those who lost their faith—
citing the Qur'an, he proclaims with trembling face,
"accept your fate, for this is Allah's will."

around the globe theologians debate:
some saying this is the way it's always been—
there's no theology here just tectonics
and humans in nature's path;
others surmising it's all because of the fall,
whatever that's supposed to mean;
others declaring God has the power
to save and destroy
to give life or not
if that is his will and way;
and still others imagining it could be
God is taking us away to a better place—
not in one apocalyptic gulp but in measured scoops

tell that to the stunned stumbling under torrid sun
who have nowhere to find the lights that left them

*

the sea was calm before the throne
          where millions were gathered—
archangels, angels, the living creatures,
          souls and souls and souls and souls—
welcoming the children carried to their shores
          on broken boats, seasoaked debris, and junks.

Children heard the song of those annulating the throne:

"Blessed is the only God,
          the Lord of wind and sea,
the only One having immortality
          and breathing it as living love and life.

You are the only One inhabiting light as Light,
          light no one has really seen or could ever know,
the One who creates darkness and brilliance,
          who can inhabit either as sun or shade,
the One who gives life, breath, and being,
          who alone shrouds the secrets of meaning
too deep, too dreadful, too awesome, too high
          for any to comprehend on this side of Light.
You are brute Beauty and awful Glory,
          the Bright behind every gloom,
the shade and sun; you shadow and illumine."

*

the man was spewed out from tumbling darkness
and slammed on shore like a shell breaking its soul
He found himself naked before the Spirit Lord
who asked: "does the sea have boundaries I haven't set?
can you tell the surging waves to stop?
have you entered into the ocean's fountains?

have you climbed deep sea mountains?
have you been to the gates of Hades
and peered down the throat of the abyss?
can you say where light is born?
can you tell me where darkness dawns?
can you dawn one morning and douse the sun
at evening in the wet horizon?
can you make each wave rise surge bellow
brim trim peel curl crash froth fizz and disappear?"

Riverscapes

32a. between the river and the sea

Waccamaw Neck, South Carolina

between the running river and the sea
on a thin neck of southern earth
creatures still fly free and roam—
it's home to the puma spotted in the woods,
the red fox with white tipped tail
I glanced prancing from glen to glen;
the pileated woodpecker drilling the pine;
the wild boar foraging the island's bush;
the hoot owl rotating its head to look
at me, the strangest member of the brood
lacking wings, claws, talons, and coat.
Yet I have eyes to catch beauty's flight
rushing past me like streams and waves,
and I am brave not to kill what's left of life.

32b. roll Spirit, river my soul

Wacammaw River, South Carolina

roll Spirit, river my soul,
rock smooth, pull, groove,
move me into zen again, send,
let then be now and now then.
as this water opens to revelation
my interpretation bends around
rooting cypress, glaring gators,
old rice plantations, savannahs
sucking summer out of sun.

roll Spirit, river my mind,
let my peace find your soul
glistening in daylight splendor,
let the ever of everlasting break
upon me with the energy of beauty,
let the river hawks fly my thoughts
into sundown serenity and eve
let me cleave to open moments
as I leave behind blind hesitation

33a. slow beauty, slow circle

the marsh near Pawleys Island, South Carolina

Mirroring mackerel skies, flocculate clouds, sun so bright
it shouts, a cirrus seacreek annulates Pawleys Island,
            a corolla round a cay that's been hurricaned
to death and resurrects. Each sunrise is breath.
The oscillating tide pushes the creek high, pulls it low
            in pulmonary flow, sucking sea air into its throat,
exhaling a scent so pungent it's poignant.
I sit creekside hearing breaking waves off to my east,
waves that have beached spermwhales, buried billions
    of unsouled shells, broken bodies into sand,
and hurled at man more mysteries than explanations.
On a sunworn dock reaching into this savannah,
I admire a swallowtail hanging summersun on amaranth
its wings shutting, papyrus pressed, and flinging open
an aperture into ever slowness. A bullfrog not about
to move the day bellows in sawgrass not hurrying sun
or shade, as yonder I eye a gator gliding as quiet as time,
his stare never aging, his eyes not fearing that I am.
            I spot a goldeyed snowy egret ghosting forward
with slow step in silent shallows bending its sigmoid neck
in half a circle; the other penciled by imagination.
It's all a slow circle drawn diurnal,
a continual annulating in euphotic waters where
acropetal auroles appear everywhere from nowhere.
I didn't throw a stone or cast a line or dip my toe.
And there were no raindrops I could feel.
My thoughts drift into shades of brown smeared across
the marsh lit by summersun burning out the cusp of day.
Does anything here imagine anything else?
I wish I had no other mind as I sit here watching
lightfall spring native night, moonshadows crawl around,
and stars birthed in some novae billion lightyears past
just now being grasped.

33b. going to seed

the marsh near Pawleys Island, South Carolina

the head heavies to neck bending,
and uglies, turning autumn ash—
don't despise those unslightly facial hairs—
they're but semeia of transfiguration:
my soul is unburdening, puffing bright,
splitting into a million seeded tufts
waiting to catch wind—once blown apart
I'll be scattered, sown, and grown for good

just try to drown me—my corky drift fruit
will fare the sea and loft in atlantic flotsam.
or burn me to the ground—I'll crack open
bright fireweed seed in a whirling cloud.
smart colors unfurl, unveiled designs astound—
the seed is revelation that life wills life on.

34a. catch the meaning

River around Seabrook Island, South Carolina

I just missed the hissing bobcat bounding in the bush
and a siting of puma roused me
to search on the morrow he didn't appear.
the marsh hummed as always with cicada strum
the stream sung as ever over fallen rock—
if I were spirit everywhere I could watch.

other signs are fixed as sun moon stars
their constancy carries the flight of day
and beaches boundaries for my swelling thoughts.
wave after wave connects the drifting continents
where natives spot the cheeta slinking past the dark
and fishers catch the meaning of a broken net.

34b. a certain presence

River around Seabrook Island, South Carolina

every living river exudes a certain presence:
in the infinitude of the moment
liquid quiddity passes into consciousness,
aquatic apotheosis oozes, an aura glows,
and its quintessence flows unutterably real,
quiet as sunrise, and quick (it can't be caught)
nor can it be lost on those who know
and touch the revelation in person—
it's like feeling water pass through to the next
moment of now; it's animal, primal, unfinal,
palpable for an instant until another present.

35a. speak peace

mountain stream, Colorado

elk bound softpawed through white aspen
black bear paw rainbow trout from streams

all ears to the symphonic river
that smooths rocks and signals sun
all eyes to the hungry hunted
who escape the fleet, swoop, and tongue

an unburrowed groundhog spies enemies
a magpie glides on upward draft

all ears to the snaredrum thunder
that scares mares and spooks rain
all eyes to the hoarhead peaks
that speak peace to those insane

35b. watersound

Colorado River

too much is made of meaning, too little is wrung from sound
rhyme is defunct, uncool, rhythm untapped and snared
moderns can't hear rivers carving canyons
seas sanding shores
continents shifting in water
glaciers moving poles
(their sound signifies nothing)
but it is not noise—no—when spheres sing to spheres
and deep calls to deep in language we can't fathom
the motion is music
the music is word
the word is spoken
when the speaker can be heard
it slithers mississippi and colorado curves
it creeps sahara slowly under the utter sun
as rivers become oceans and seas become poems

36a. depths

Colorado River

a stripe upon a canyon wall
          where rivers forced a sear
the tracing is not just and square
as limned by some carpenter
it dips
          jags
                              disappears
merges with other lines
then reappears
                    in different form
it bears no record of what has lived
only what has been

no one examining the wear
will note the stroke of being cut
          all groans are garbled in untold rush
downward to the sea, then hushed
how
mute
were
the
deaths
that
forged
these
awful
depths

36b. descent

Starved Rock, Illinois

each tier
marks
a millennium
in this canyon
            carved by ancient rivers
it was home to Illini
I've never seen.

today I stand
where they stood
but can't fathom
what they suffered
when they chose
starvation over
surrender

I've stepped
where they've stepped
I've slept
where they last laid their heads
but I don't know their names
and they've never thought of mine

time has not
distanced us

descent has

37a. visions of rivers

there is a river in our thoughts, our spirits
a river that streams from the mouth of God
a river that flows from our deepest dreams

Ezekiel saw a river rushing from God's throne
Jesus promised a river to all who drink from him
John envisioned a river winding through new Jersualem

measure it to the ankles; measure it to the knees;
measure it to the stomach; measure it to the mouth—
swim and drink, float and sink, roll in the rush

plush greens line its banks, fruit trees root its edges,
fishermen wade its waters, fish its plentiful shallows,
children romp its inlets, skip stones across its face

dogs chase box turtles scurrying its muddy shores,
dragonflies skim its surface, gators sun themselves,
canoers paddle the rapids, steering through the rocks

God is alive in the river, on the river, through the river,
Spirit is fountain, flow, course, brook, and stream—
the river of the water of life is essence of our being

37b. midwest streams, dolphin dreams

the Midwest rolls in gray horizons
too far from either shore to matter
farms slice the landscape soaked with muddy streams
spotted with wet woods and snaking streams
Ohio to Kansas lays flat like a brown slab on canvas
a pointillist would have dabbed it with dull yellow, drab green
a surrealist as in some celestial dream above the plain
would have shaped gleaming dolphins riding aqua pipelines
in tandom with windborne surfers splashing crystal doplets
down on the dull brown as if it were sunset beach—
but Midwesterners are realists
who know Malibu is out of reach
they put cities on the map
where weary travelers have to stop

38a Chicora speaks

Winyah Bay, South Carolina

The year was 1521, before any colonization had begun.
Spanish slave raiders captured sixty men and women
of the coastal tribes who thrived in Pawleys Island,
Winyah Bay, and along the waterways where I live now.
These tribes, known as the Chicora and Wacammaw,
worshiped the one Great Spirit, Wakan Tanka.

Among the newly baptized natives, Francisco de Chicora
was taken to be the slave of a judge in Hispaniola.
This owner, Lucas Vazquez de Ayllon, sailed him to Spain,
where Chicora thoroughly learned the native tongue.
He told stories of homeland wealth of splendid scope
to Martyr and Oveido, who spread the news through Europe.

Chicora returned a few years later with Ayllon's expedition
that founded San Miguel de Gualdape, America's first colonization.
Their fluent translator and trusted guide, he steered them
to Hobcaw in Winyah Bay, then escaped with other captive Indians.
Fooled by Chicora's myths, the colony hoped for bonanza,
but found only a restless sea and sun-soaked savanna.

38b. Black Elk speaks

Little Powder River, Wyoming

So many since then have become grass upon the hills
under the bitten moon of hungry winter.
Wasichus' treaty said our land would be ours
as long as grasses grow and waters flow—
you can see it's not the grass and river who've forgotten.

Our men are dark in the lostness of their eyes.
they've dried out like parched corn, smoked tobacco ash,
strewn buffalo skulls. They hobble with their canes
looking to earth for something they can't remember.

I had a dream that's wiser than waking.
I saw the shapes of all things spirit,
the shapes of all shape as they breathe together
in the great circle, the hoop of awakening.

I saw the face of earth's day appearing,
where bison roam the plain like cloud shadow
where forests are thick as bear fur
and where all the twoleggeds and fourleggeds
breathe the yellow air afraid of nothing.

39a. papyrus maker

Nile River

“with water’s tongue upon her mouth
silt her form at floodtime
runoff’s sweat from out her flesh—
she is the whole, the whole she is
for she is the Nile, mother of all”
he sang in the papyri bending wind

wading the flood, he hacked stalks
hauled them to shore, peeled stems
sliced thin strips from pith
layed them footlong side by side
slightly overlapping, superimposing
more oozing strips at right angles

he left tired as a dung bettle
that pushed the sun around all day
and saw a falcon overhead with breasts
dark as evening and downy shadows
he gazed at the moon lighting the way home
and imagined the face of an orbiting god

in the morning he returned
to the papyri layed out in rows
and beat the strips with mallets
he pummeled papyrus like sunstrokes
till the cells interlocked into married sheets
he polished and marketed

a scribe in Oxyrhynchus penned
recto and verso with majuscules
calligraphing heavy and thin strokes
the memoirs of him who had penned
the story of one who wrote more with a life
than men can invent with lampblack ink

39b. Ezekiel's vision

By the Kebar River

A sight! light! Illumination pooling outward
in nimbus moons, in concentric circles.
Must be Spirit-God at the core.
Do I see Zoa surrounding the Throne?
Could they be radiating Deity?
There are angels encompassing them
and other creations expanding in glowing halo.
Surrounding the throne are Zoa sprouting cherubic wings
with surreal eyes, faces, pionions,
and hands under outstretched wings
touching each other all around.
They countenance changeable faces,
sprout wings of angels, move wherever the living Spirit roves
never veering from their spirited course
these Zoa speeding lightning are like roving wheels
by which the Divine wings worlds,
takes flight, finds face, and pilgrims space.

Four Zoa (like cherubim I've seen on the Temple's curtains)
surround the throne, full of eyes front and behind.
The first Zoa looks lion, the second Zoa ox,
the third Zoa countenances a human face,
and fourth Zoa an awesome eagle.
All four Zoa have eyes inside and all around.
The eyes in the back must see Him Who Was
the ever-existing original Energy,
the creative Creator, designer, and progenitor.
The eyes inside see Him Who Is
the quintessential zoe, the source of life and being,
the One whose beginnings never end.
The eyes in the front see Him Who Is To Come
in the parousia of paradise in new Jerusalem.

The empyrean erupts in ferocious stormwinds,
dreadful clouds flashing electrum.
Lightning stuns, then brightness blinds my eyes,
as spirits flash in the solemn sanctuary
with sacred smoke. Glory is terrible.

The fluttering of wings is ocean of sound,
voice almighty, the roar of rushing armies.
I hear but see nothing. My eyes strain
against the unearthly brightness out of which
eyes look back at me. Multiple eyes—
lion-fierce, eagle-piercing, oxen-mean,
human-gleam—more exotic than any sphinx
or ogling griffin I've sighted in Babylonian temples.

They unfurl eyes front, back, inside, around:
(Imminence, Preeminence, Emmanance, Omnipresence—
all creatures are forever seen by him.)
The eyes of the Zoa palanquin the roaming Glory.
Now I eye God's rolling wheels—
as God (it must be) expands his reach and breadth,
they flash and flame, moving wherever Spirit roves,
never veering from their spirited course.

Pilgriming illimitable space with God-eyes
round as wheels and wide as morning suns,
they speed light-quick through everylivingthing,
peering into my darkened thoughts that want
to hide as much from light as God.
Was I raptured to the Throne?
Is it monsters or metaphors I catch in flight?

Above his head is a lapis lazuli throne
and high above it human likeness;
I see a son of man in glowing glory.
From the waist upwards he is flaming fire;
from the waist downward, all aflame.
His eyes are ignited with burning blaze.
His feet glow as burnished bronze.

His voice sounds roaring surf and wind.
His mouth is a two-edged flashing sword,
and his face effulges in full sun's strength.
I quiver. terrified. shrink. slump.
Sacred splendid radiance surrounds him
like a rainbow bursting rainsoaked clouds.

I hear ocean voice from the throne proclaim:
"Behold, the invincible Son of Man!
As sure as new heavens and earth are coming,
God's Warrior, as carried on cherubim wings
will incarnate among the sons of men!
Heaven's glories, sacredness, and verve
will kingdom earth, will saint humans,
and angel what's serpentine, sinister, and sin."

40. summer has run rivers into ocean

Epilogue Poem

It's late October—summer has run rivers into ocean.
I get high watching monarchs migrate south,
tuning circadian antennae to the sun.
It's not yet my winter, nor ever theirs.
I escape the cold for as long as sun grows shadows.
I resort to dreams of waves as strong as autumn
and beachcombers raking the shore.
I want more, much more to break my way;
so I will wade in and out of shivering waters,
not fearing that death delays.

Author Biographical Note:

Philip Comfort studied Greek and English at the Ohio State University (where he received an MA), then went on to get a doctorate in literary interpretation from the University of South Africa. He has been a senior editor at Tyndale House Publishers for nearly 25 years, and he has taught English, Religion, and Greek at several colleges, including Wheaton College, Columbia International University, and Coastal Carolina University. He has authored several academic books and two novels, Rescued Retriever and Caribbean Castaways. He was the New Testament coordinating editor and one of the translators for the New Living Translation, which has sold over 20 million copies. He lives in Pawleys Isalnd, South Carolina, with his beloved wife, Georgia.

His love of poetry began when he was a teenager. He emulated the style of Dylan Thomas in his early years, then he went on to develop his own style. His favorite poets include John Donne, Emily Dickinson, and Gerard Manley Hopkins. He (with Daniel Partner) compiled a a volume entitled A Poem A Day (Lion Hudson, England); it contains 365 poems of spiritual poets, with commentary. Then he wrote Spirit Journey, a collection of autobiographical poems, reflecting on his journey from events like Woodstock, the Kent State shootings (May 4, 1970), to his wife's successful battle with cancer in the 1990s. She has been a continual source of inspiration to him throughout his life. His other two books of poems were inspired by the ocean: Oceanic and Seascapes, which was nominated for the Pushcart Award.